MYZONE

BOYFRIENDS AND STUFF

ANITA GANERI

FIRST PUBLISHED IN 2010 BY
FRANKLIN WATTS
338 EUSTON ROAD
LONDON NW1 3BH

FRANKLIN WATTS AUSTRALIA
LEVEL 17/207 KENT STREET
SYDNEY NSW 2000

COPYRIGHT © FRANKLIN WATTS 2010

SERIES EDITOR: ADRIAN COLE
ART DIRECTOR: JONATHAN HAIR
DESIGN: BLUE PAW DESIGN
PICTURE RESEARCH: DIANA MORRIS
CONSULTANT: FIONA M. COLLINS,
    ROEHAMPTON UNIVERSITY

ALL RIGHTS RESERVED.

A CIP CATALOGUE RECORD OF THIS BOOK
IS AVAILABLE FROM THE BRITISH LIBRARY

ISBN: 978 0 7496 9564 4

DEWEY CLASSIFICATION: 306.7

ACKNOWLEDGEMENTS:
Yuri Arcurs/Fotolia: 4,5. Atelier 22/Shutterstock.: 6. Eric Audas/Alamy: 43t. Galina Barskaya/Shutterstock: 21b. bebo tm: 37t. bobbieo/istockphoto: 18. bphotographer/Shutterstock: 40. Phil Date/Shutterstock: 19t. David Davis/Shutterstock: 36. Denkou Images/Alamy: 17. Tony DiMaio/Rex Features: 15b. Hammond Dovi/istockphoto: 19b. East/istockphoto: 39. Elena Elisseeva/Shutterstock: 24. Erics/Shutterstock: 7b. Jamie Evans/istockphoto: 13br. Facebook tm: 36t. Roxy Fer/Shutterstock: 12br. Golden Pixels LLC/Shutterstock: 27. David J Green/Alamy: 31b. Gerville Hall/istcokphoto: 33. Jiri Hera/Shutterstock: 41b, 42t. Alex Hinds/ Shutterstock: 11. Image Source/Alamy: 7c. Cristian Lazzari/istcokphoto: 37. Rick Becker-Leckrone/Shutterstock: 26. Rick Legg/istockphoto: 28. Sean Locke/istockphoto: 38. Stan Locke/istockphoto: 9. Cat London/istcokphoto: 20. microimages/fotolia: 21t. Monkey Business Images/Shutterstock: 13bl, 25, 34. franz pfluegl/istockphoto: 29. Pidjoe/istockphoto: 30. Tatiana Popova/Shutterstock: 16. Chris Rout/Alamy: 22. Chris Schmidt/istockphoto: 43b. Amanda Schwab/Rex Features: 14, 15t. Ian Shaw/Alamy: 31t. Liz van Steenburgh/Shutterstock: 12bl. Jason Stitt/istockphoto: 10. Twitter tm: 37c. Claudia Vega/istockphoto: 32. Jacob Wackerhausen/istockphoto: 8. Tracey Whiteside/Shutterstock: 35t. Winterling/istockphoto: 42b. David Young-Wolff/Alamy: 23. Lisa F Young/istockphoto: 35b. Zorani/istockphoto: 41t.

EVERY ATTEMPT HAS BEEN MADE TO CLEAR COPYRIGHT. SHOULD THEIR BE ANY INADVERTENT OMISSION PLEASE APPLY TO THE PUBLISHER FOR RETIFICATION

PRINTED IN CHINA

FRANKLIN WATTS IS A DIVISION OF
HACHETTE CHILDREN'S BOOKS,
AN HACHETTE UK COMPANY.
WWW.HACHETTE.CO.UK

Please note: every effort has been made by the Publishers to ensure that the websites in this book contain no inappropriate or offensive material. However, because of the nature of the Internet, it is impossible to guarantee that the contents of these sites will not be altered. We strongly advise that Internet access is supervised by a responsible adult.

VALE OF GLAMORGAN LIBRARY	
03899259	
HJ	21-Dec-2010
J306.7	£11.99

LOOK OUT FOR...

6	LOVE IS A FOUR LETTER WORD
8	IS THIS LOVE?
10	COPING WITH CRUSHES
12	PERFECT BOYFRIEND QUIZ
14	SUPERSTAR BOYFRIENDS
16	VALENTINE'S DAY
18	TOP TEN TURN-OFFS
20	FIRST DATE GUIDE
22	PERFECT KISS GUIDE
24	BOYFRIEND BUST-UPS
26	ARE YOU A GREAT MATE?
28	MAKING FRIENDS
30	PAL PROBLEMS
32	PEER PRESSURE
34	BEING BULLIED
36	SOCIAL NETWORKING
40	SERIOUS STUFF
44	GLOSSARY
45	MORE WEBSITES
46	INDEX

Words highlighted in the text can be found in the glossary.

"Hi, welcome to **MY ZONE**. I've been collecting all the best picks for this edition, from boyfriend tips to best friend break-ups. Looking for love? Fallen out with your mates? Then you've come to the right place."

Anita x

LOVE IS A FOUR LETTER WORD

Love or hate them, boys are a big part of your life, especially as you're growing up. Suddenly, you find your feelings changing. Boys you wouldn't have wasted your time on before start looking like boyfriend material. You find yourself fancying someone, and before you know it, you're in L-O-V-E!

♥ Daydreaming about boys is fun – but what about when it gets serious?

WEBtag

You will see WEBtags throughout this book. Many websites feature more information about the articles inside, videos and up-to-date news and blogs.

But boyfriends aren't the only people in your universe. Friends are really important, too. But what happens when you fall out? And what about making friends on-line, and making sure you stay safe? Inside this book, you will find loads of advice to help you with friends and boyfriends. Plus there are lots of views to think and chat about, and some health advice too.

Friends love sharing the latest gossip and photos!

7

IS THIS LOVE?

You catch his eye across a crowded room and your stomach goes crazy! Your palms feel sweaty; your mouth goes dry. Are you falling ill? No, it sounds as if you're falling in love!

Experts reckon there are three phases of being in love:

1 Fancying: you love his gorgeous blond hair and blue eyes.

2 Attraction: you fall head over heels in love with him.

3 Attachment: you want to spend the rest of your life with him.

Falling in love for the first time can be great but, actually, most early relationships only last for a few months. Don't worry. You'll soon find yourself falling in love again with someone else.

It's official! You can't help yourself falling in love! Between 9–14 years old, you go through **puberty**. This is the time when your body changes from a child's into an adult's, so that you can have babies one day – if you want them.

All this happens because powerful chemicals, called **hormones**, start whizzing around your body. They change how you look and how you feel, so you suddenly find yourself attracted to people in a way you've never been before.

http://www.seventeen.com/love/advice

WEBtag Lots of articles and boyfriend tips.

COPING WITH CRUSHES

Got a killer crush on the hottest boy in your class? But he doesn't even notice you're alive? Here's our guide to spotting the signs of a crush and tips for coping if he doesn't fancy you back.

HOW TO SPOT A CRUSH

- You can't stop thinking about your crush.
- You spend hours searching for 'clues' to prove you and your crush are the perfect match.
- You only tell your best friend who your crush is.

- You desperately want your crush to notice you but it's soooo embarrassing when he does.
- You spend even more hours imagining what a future with your crush would be like.

FEELING CRUSHED?

Living with a crush isn't easy. It's hard to concentrate, eat and sleep. Here are some top tips for coping…

1. Take time to daydream about your crush but don't let this get in the way of real life.

2. Take up a hobby or throw yourself into school work to distract yourself.

3. Don't forget about your friends. Make sure you still spend high-quality time with them.

4. Don't worry. Crushes can seem overwhelming but they usually only last for a few weeks.

DID YOU KNOW?
You can have a crush on anyone. It can be someone you know like a friend's older brother or sister, or a cool teacher. Or it can be someone you're never even likely to meet, like a famous footballer or pop star.

http://www.sugarscape.com/channel/lads

WEBtag Gossip pages featuring the latest celeb crushes.

PERFECT BOYFRIEND QUIZ

Always falling for the wrong boy? Not sure which type's your type? Don't worry – we're here to help. Find your dream boyfriend with our magic match-making quiz...

1 What is your personality?

A Wacky and fun
B Loud and lively
C Hardworking and clever
D Quiet and reserved

2 What are your favourite tunes?

A Rock
B RnB and Dance
C Pop or Classical
D Indie or Alternative

3. What do you always have in your bag?
- **A** iPod
- **B** Lip gloss
- **C** A book
- **D** Sketch pad

4. What is your favourite fashion style?
- **A** Scruffy chic
- **B** Cool and sporty
- **C** Smart-casual
- **D** Gothic cool

5. What is your best feature?
- **A** Your sense of humour
- **B** Your looks
- **C** Your brains
- **D** Your individuality

Mostly As – Dreamy boys like you, they love music and have a laid-back approach to life. They can get caught up in daydreams though.

Mostly Bs – Bad boys They like looking good and know what they want. But behind their cool shades and huge egos, they're really quite sensitive.

Mostly Cs – Brainy boys They like you because you're clever and easy to talk to, just like them. And you think there's more to life than your make-up bag.

Mostly Ds – Sensitive boys They like to do their own thing, but when you get to know them they can be friends for life. They get hurt easily though.

SUPERSTAR BOYFRIENDS

If you find yourself with a massive celeb crush, don't worry, you're not alone. Here are just a few of the superstar boyfriends who send girls weak at the knees.

http://www.jonas-brothers.com

WEBtag Jonas Brothers' official website.

Jonas Brothers (from left to right, Kevin, Nick and Joe)
Boyfriend rating: "Hunky and hot"
The superstar Jonas Brothers don't just look good. They're also brilliant actors and singers so they could sing you a soppy love song while you look deep into their eyes…

WEBtag Corbin Bleu pages on IMDb, featuring an image gallery and video clips.

http://www.imdb.com/name/nm0088298

Corbin Bleu
Boyfriend rating: "Sooooo cool"
Totally gorgeous Corbin shot to fame in *High School Musical*. He sings, dances and acts – is there no end to this boyfriend's talents? And there's more good news, girls. Corbin likes cooking, loves animals and he's a **Pisces**, so he's bound to have a sensitive side.

Justin Bieber
Boyfriend rating: "Cute, cute, cute"
Canadian teen pop sensation Justin already has girls falling at his feet. With his mix of pretty-boy looks and streetwise **attitude** he's mobbed by thousands of fans, sparking 'Bieber fever' wherever he goes. Put on his music and pretend he's all yours!

VALENTINE'S DAY

Traditionally, 14th February is the day people send cards (or emails, texts and tweets) and flowers to those they love. But do you think V-Day's a brilliant time for romance? Or do you hate it with a passion?

LOVE IT!

HATE IT!

It's a bit **OTT** but it's still fun to see if anyone sends you a card.

It's a great chance to show someone you love them.

It's a complete rip-off – the cards and flowers are overpriced!

It's just an excuse to be disgustingly gushy! Gross!

DID YOU KNOW?
The original St Valentine lived in Italy in the first century CE. Legend says that he carried out secret weddings, against the Emperor's orders. He was put in jail and later beheaded, but not before he sent the first Valentine's card to the jailor's daughter.

VALENTINE'S DAY SURVIVAL GUIDE

Before you go rushing off to check the post (again), here are some top tips for surviving Valentine's Day...

1 Practise your 'couldn't-care-less' look, just in case:
A someone sends you a big bunch of roses
B you don't get anything at all.

2 If you haven't got a date lined up, arrange to go out with your mates instead, or have a girly night in.

3 If you're single, don't spend the day moping about and feeling sorry for yourself. Buy yourself some flowers or chocs.

4 If no one sends you a card, cheat! Buy a card, sign it with lots of hearts and kisses and make sure that everyone sees it.

http://www.history.com/topics/valentines-day

WEBtag Valentine's Day facts from History.com.

TOP TEN TURN-OFFS

What do boys really want in a girlfriend? We've been out asking boys what gets on their nerves about girls. We've used their responses to put together this quick guide…

1 Taking too long to get ready. Why do girls have to spend so much time in front of the mirror?

2 Slating our mates. Even if they are losers, we like them and that's what matters.

3 Trying to change us. Telling us what to wear and what music/films/books to like.

4 Getting **jealous** when we look at another girl. It's only looking!

> I hate it when you go out with a girl and they think everyone's looking at them. They're not! Get over it!

18

5 Pretending to like football. We can see straight through it.

6 Always talking, and telling their friends everything.

7 Getting mad when they ask you for your honest opinion… and you give it.

> Girls always have to tell their mates everything. You give her a kiss and suddenly the whole world knows.

8 Always going on about how cool/funny/good-looking their ex-boyfriends were.

9 Bringing up stuff you said ages ago and using it against you.

10 10 PDAs. Yes, Public Displays of Affection (kissing, holding hands, cuddling). Enough said.

> I went out with this girl in my year. It was fun to start with, but then she wouldn't let me out of her sight. Too clingy!

FIRST DATE GUIDE

So he's finally asked you out. Now the panic begins. Just seeing your crush makes you blush, so how are you going to deal with a date? The secret is to be yourself and have fun.

To avoid dating disaster, here's our fool-proof guide...

Be cool and **confident**, but don't go OTT and say or do anything you might regret later. Besides, you don't want to scare him off.

Anita says: stay safe on a date – tell people where you are going, who you're with and when you'll be back.

Where to go...

- Have a plan, then you won't waste time working out where to go. Pick something you'll enjoy. Here are a few ideas:

- Grab a coffee
- Have a picnic
- Go for a pizza
- Watch a film
- Go ice skating
- Go bowling
- Take a walk in the park

20

What to wear...

○ Choose something that looks good and feels comfortable.

○ Don't use a first date to try out a brand-new fashion look.

○ Dress for the occasion. Heels won't be great if you'll be doing lots of walking.

> It's fine for a girl to make the first move and ask a boy out. Just don't make a song and dance out of it, or embarrass him in front of his mates.

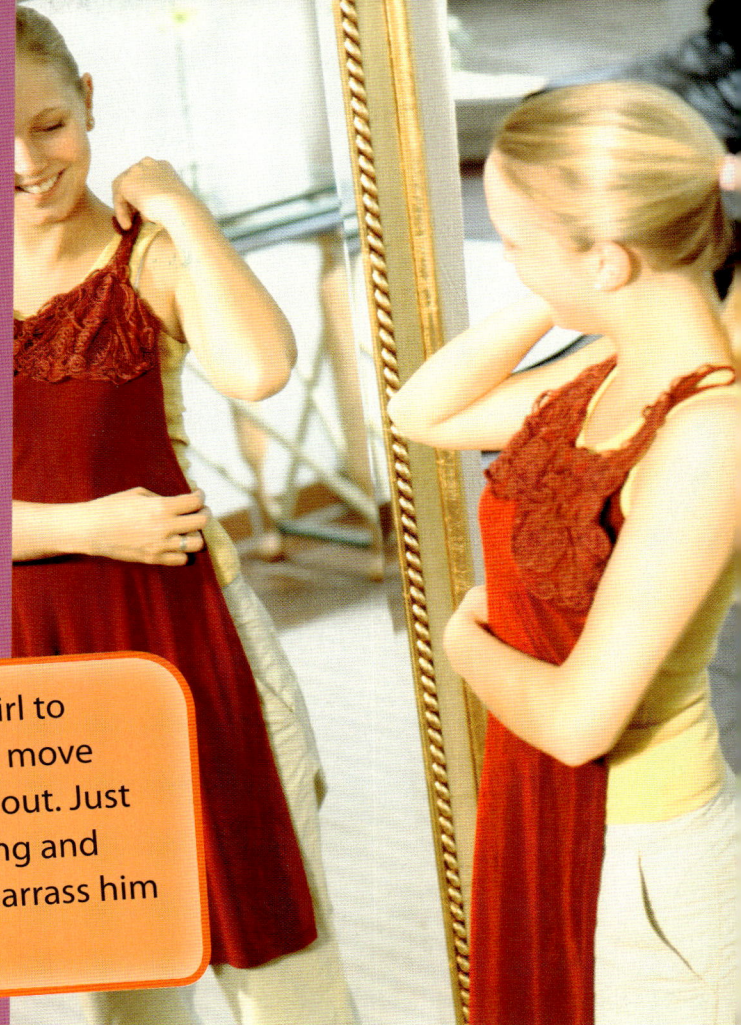

What to talk about...

○ Have a few topics of conversation ready beforehand. For example, ask which films/bands/sports/TV programmes he likes.

○ Don't worry about trying to be cool or funny.

○ Sound and act confident and you can get away with anything.

PERFECT KISS GUIDE

Your date is going well. You're holding hands. You look into each other's eyes... Is your first kiss looming?

First kisses are exciting but you're also worried you'll get it all wrong. Stay calm. You'll find it comes naturally, especially if you follow our top tips for lips...

DID YOU KNOW?
The record for the longest kiss is held by James Belshaw and Sophia Severin from the UK. Their super-long snog lasted for 31 hours, 30 minutes and 30 seconds!

http://www.teenissues.co.uk/FirstKissTips.htm

WEBtag More first kiss tips and other teen advice.

22

Kissing with confidence

1. Lean in and tilt your head so you don't bash noses.
2. Close your eyes so you don't go cross-eyed.
3. Part your lips slightly and press them against his.
4. As your lips make contact, purse them slightly so they're soft and relaxed.
5. Keep your first kiss short and sweet – around 10 seconds long.

Top tips for hot lips...

- Have a mint or breath freshener handy. Bad breath is a real turn-off.
- Some boys are shy, so take the lead. Kiss him lightly on the cheek first.
- Only kiss someone if you think they're ready and that they'll kiss back.
- Don't kiss someone with a cold, chapped lips or a cold sore.
- Your first kiss should be a private moment, so find somewhere to yourselves.
- Leave tongues until later – you don't want to scare him off.

♥ Relax! Don't get too stressed out about the details. And, anyway, practice makes perfect.

BOYFRIEND BUST-UPS

Being dumped can be heartbreaking, especially if you really like someone. And doing the dumping can be nearly as bad. You've emailed me some of your own real-life relationship no-gos.

DUMPED BY TEXT!

I got dumped by text and I was furious. He said he didn't have time to talk to me because he had to go to football practice, but he thought we'd be better off as mates. I was really upset but my best friend said who wants to be mates with a coward like him. I don't!

If you're planning to dump someone, pick your moment. Don't tell him before an exam or in front of his mates. Work out beforehand why you want to ditch him, then tell him straight. Fobbing him off with excuses will only make things worse.

SECOND CHANCE?

I told my boyfriend he was dumped. Then I saw him with another girl and I wanted him back. But he said he just wants to be mates. I reckon he still fancies me, so I'm going to ask him if he wants to go to see a film. Then I'll know for sure.

STILL INTO HIS EX?

My boyfriend is always comparing me to his ex and going on about how amazing she was. And I'm getting really fed up with it. I asked him about it and he told me I was imagining it. But if he does it again, he's definitely dumped!

RIGHT FIRST TIME?

I used to go out with a boy, but things didn't work out so we ended it. Then, recently, we ended up kissing at a party. Afterwards, we arranged to meet up but since then, he's been **blanking** me. He's either got someone else or has changed his mind.

http://www.girlslife.com/category/guys.aspx

WEBtag Lots of relationship advice and stories.

ARE YOU A GREAT MATE?

Everyone knows that friends are really important. But what sort of pal are you? Try our quick quiz to see if you've got what it takes to be a great mate. Just answer 'yes' or 'no' to these questions, then add up your scores.

1 Do you share the same tastes in music/movies/fashion?

2 If your friends have got a problem, are you a good listener?

3 If you've got a big decision to make, do you ask your friends' advice?

4 If your friends tell you a secret, do you keep it?

♥ Great friends stick together through good and bad times – and may be friends for life.

5 Can you and your friends disagree about something, without falling out?

6 After a **tiff**, do you and your friends make up, then forget about it?

7 Do you always remember your friends' birthdays?

8 Can you tell when your friends are upset, without asking?

9 When your friends are ill, do you check up on them?

10 If your friends want to do something stupid, do you tell them?

Now give this quiz to your best friend and see how she/he does! It's a good way of finding out lots of cool stuff about each other.

Your score:

1–2 yes's: Fair-weather friend. Your friendships need work! You don't seem to care much about your friends at all. Try spending more time with them.

3–6 yes's: Good friend. There are still barriers between you and your friends, but you're well on the way to being a great mate and you know that friendships work both ways.

7–10 yes's: Best mate. Congratulations! You really care about your friends. Just be careful that your friendships don't become too clingy or suffocating.

27

MAKING FRIENDS

Making new friends can be tricky, especially if you've moved house or started at a new school – or perhaps your best friend has moved away.

Here are our five top tips for making friends if you want some new pals, but don't know how…

Stand tall! Looking confident is really important, even if you don't feel it. Stand up tall, with your shoulders back and your arms by your sides. You'll be amazed at how different you feel.

Make the first move Don't just sit in a corner and wait for people to come to talk to you. Take a deep breath and chat to someone. It can help to have something ready to say.

Keep smiling If you look friendly and **approachable**, people will want to approach you and get to know you. Being likeable gets people on side and builds an instant connection.

webtag Friends, family and mental health advice

http://www.gurl.com/topics/friendsfamily

Join in Go to something like an after-school club or take up a sport you like. You'll meet people who share a similar interest and, chances are, you'll become good friends.

Be patient! It can take a while to make new friends, so be patient. The more people you meet, the more friends you're likely to make. You can't have too many!

Remember, even people who seem to be the centre of attention, and loving it, are not always as cool and confident as they look.

PAL PROBLEMS

Friendships can be hard work. One minute you're best mates, the next, she's moved on to somebody else. You make up, break up and make up again. But if you've got a particular pal problem, here's the **MY ZONE** agony aunt with some advice.

Feeling left out

All my mates have boyfriends, apart from me. I feel really left out and reckon there must be something wrong with me.

First of all, there's nothing wrong with you! It doesn't matter if you haven't got a boyfriend. There's no rush and you'll meet someone when the time is right. Secondly, tell your friends you feel left out and suggest a girlie sleepover or movie night.

http://www.beinggirl.co.uk/home.php

WEBtag Packed with advice about problem friends and personal health issues.

Being mean

One of my best friends has started saying mean things about me behind my back. I'm really upset about it but don't know what to do.

Your best bet is to talk to your friend about it and find out what's going on. If she's honest and realises how much she's hurt you, you might be able to save your friendship. If not, perhaps it's time to find another friend.

Bad influence

My mum thinks my best friend is a bad **influence** on me. But I think she's great and I don't want to stop seeing her.

Don't worry, this happens a lot! Don't get cross with your mum – she's only thinking of you. Try having a chat with her to find out why she doesn't like your friend. If it's because your mum doesn't really know your friend, get the two of them together.

31

PEER PRESSURE

What if your mates try to make you do something simply because they're all doing it, even if you don't want to? This is **negative** peer pressure. (Your peers are people your own age, like your classmates.) But there's also positive peer pressure.

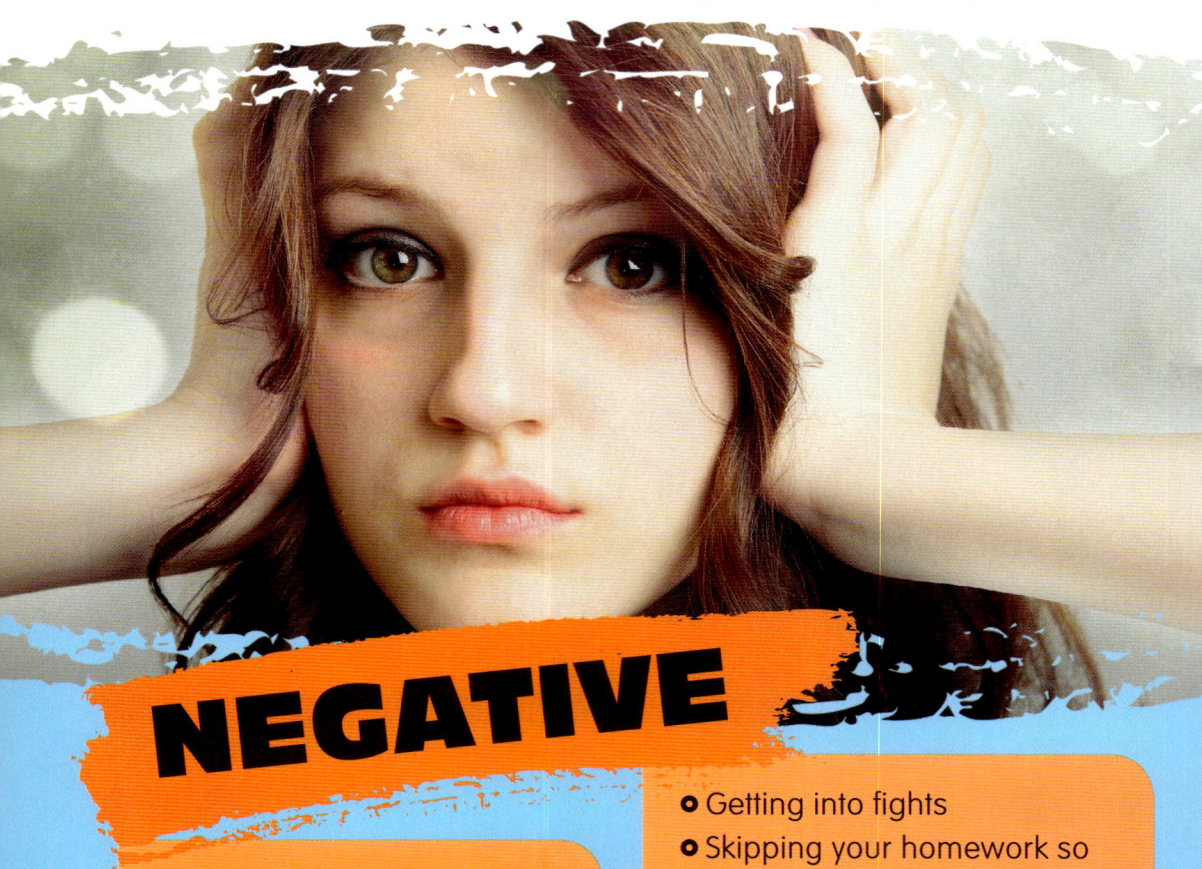

NEGATIVE

- Sneaking out of the house
- Drinking or smoking
- Stealing or shoplifting
- Picking on other people
- Getting into fights
- Skipping your homework so you can go to a party
- **Bunking off** school to go shopping
- Swearing because everyone else does

Standing up to your friends can be difficult because you worry what they'll think of you, and you want to be liked and fit in. But it's also important to be yourself and only do what you feel comfortable with. If they're real friends, they'll respect your wishes and like you for who you are.

POSITIVE

So, is peer pressure ever a good thing? You usually hear about the negative side of peer pressure, but it can be really useful when it means things like…

- Getting on with your schoolwork
- Helping a friend who's in trouble
- Eating healthily
- Doing regular exercise or sport
- Being caring to other people

http://www.thecoolspot.gov/right_to_resist.asp

WEBtag Suggestions for dealing with negative peer pressure.

33

BEING BULLIED

Bullying's a big problem. You might get called names, teased, hit, kicked or have your friends turned against you. It can happen to anyone and anywhere – at home, school, the youth club or online (see pages 38–39).

Bullying can make people very upset and unhappy, and it's NEVER okay. So, if you're being bullied, what can you do?

BEAT THE BULLIES...

- Tell someone. If you're being bullied at school, tell your teacher. Your school should have an anti-bullying **policy**. Otherwise, tell your parents or another adult you can trust.

- Keep a diary. Write down what happens and when it happens. Then you won't miss out anything important and it will help to show other people that you're telling the truth.

Remember, it's the bullies who have the problem, not you. It's hard to feel sorry for bullies, but they are often unhappy people who pick on others as a way of getting attention or making themselves feel big and powerful.

WEBtag Search 'bullying' to find out more.

http://kidshealth.org/teen

- Ignore the bully. Pretend you haven't heard them and walk away quickly to somewhere you feel safe. Bullies want to see how you react, so don't give them the satisfaction.

- Avoid the bully. As much as you can, stay out of the bully's way. This might mean walking a different way to school, and taking a pal along for company.

- Don't be a bully. If you see someone being bullied, speak out but don't bully them back. You're likely to get into trouble or worse, get hurt. Ask an adult for help (right).

SOCIAL NETWORKING

Social networking websites are a great way to make and catch up with friends. Are you online often, or couldn't you care less? Here's some info about three of the most famous sites…

facebook

Facebook® was started in 2004 by some students in the USA. Today, it's got more than 500 million users worldwide. You set up a personal **profile page**, then start adding friends. You can upload photos, join interest groups and send virtual gifts to your friends.

bebo

The name 'Bebo' stands for 'Blog Early, Blog Often'. You set up a personal profile page where you can post blogs, photos, videos and music. There's also an interactive timeline where you can display a record of special events in your life in the order they happen.

twitter

On Twitter™, you send a message called a 'tweet' of 140 characters or less in answer to the question 'What's happening?' This is sent to all of your 'followers'. In turn, you can follow other people and read their tweets. More than 50 million tweets are sent every day.

DID YOU KNOW?
In 2009, a US astronaut used Twitter™ to send updates back to Earth during the mission to repair the Hubble Space Telescope. It was the first time Twitter™ had been used in space.

CYBERBULLYING

A cyberbully is a person who sends nasty or threatening messages on the Internet or by mobile phone. Because so many young people are spending so much time online, it's a growing problem. Here's one girl's experience…

"Hi, my name's Emma and I used to love chatting to my friends online. Then, one day, I started getting messages from people saying nasty things about me. I didn't know who was sending them but I was really upset. I showed the messages to my mum and stopped using the site."

http://www.cybermentors.org.uk

WEBtag Find out more about how to talk to a cybermentor here.

"My mum got in touch with Cybermentors (see above). They're trained to help anyone who's being cyberbullied. They showed me the best way to handle things and really helped me to get my confidence back."

If you're being bullied, save any emails or texts and show them to an adult. NEVER reply to messages from people you don't know.

http://www.thinkuknow.co.uk

WEBtag Age-ranged information about online safety from CEOP.

HAPPY CHATTING GUIDE

With so many people using the Internet, it's easy for strangers to find out about you, and not always in a good way. So, it's important to stay cybersafe…

- Never give out any personal details online, such as your birthday.
- Be careful about which photos you post.
- Don't put details like addresses in a blog.
- Don't add anyone you don't know as your friend.
- Never arrange to meet people you only know online.
- Stay on the main social websites as these will be more closely regulated.

Social networking sites are great fun as long as they don't get out of hand. If you think they're taking over from your real life, cut down the time you spend on them and get out more with your actual friends.

SERIOUS STUFF

Okay, so the person you fancy fancies you back. You go on a date, hold hands and maybe have your first kiss. But in future you might need answers to some serious questions, so here's some advice about sex and stuff.

SERIOUS STUFF 1: SEXUAL TOUCHING

Exploring your own body down below is part of growing up – after all – so much is changing. As part of your relationship he might want to touch you too, and you might want to do this together. But don't feel pressurised – even if it might mean breaking up.

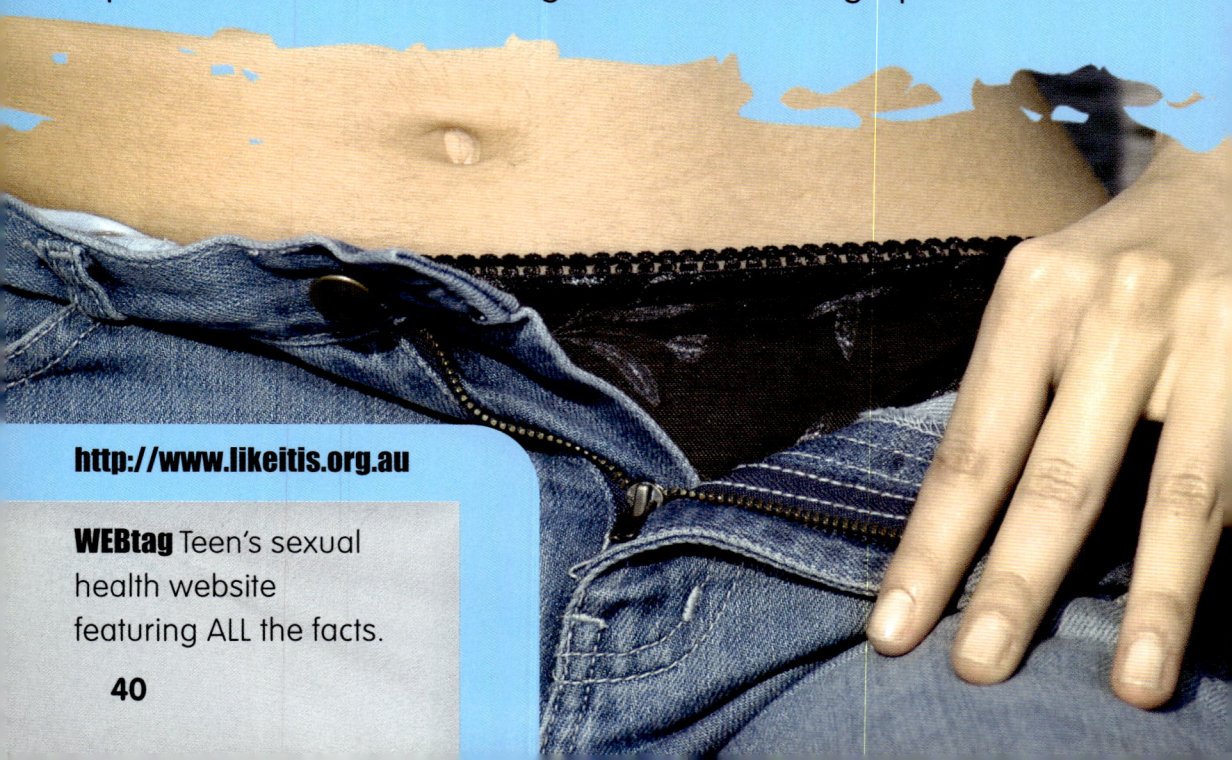

http://www.likeitis.org.au

WEBtag Teen's sexual health website featuring ALL the facts.

SERIOUS STUFF 2: SEX

You know what sex is, right? Sex (or sexual intercourse) is when a man fits his penis inside a woman's vagina, and is how babies are made. It shows their love for each other, and isn't something that should be rushed into. Sex can make you feel very good, with the right person. But it can also make you feel very bad if you have sex before you want to, or with someone you don't love or trust.

DID YOU KNOW?
It is actually against the law in the UK and most of Australia to have sex before you're 16 years old. In the USA it varies from state to state between 14 and 18 years old. You'll probably want to wait longer than that until you find someone you really love.

Don't know what this is? Turn over to find out!

SERIOUS STUFF 3: CONTRACEPTION

If a man and woman don't want to have a baby, they can take precautions to stop the woman becoming pregnant. These are called **contraception** or birth control. Here's a quick guide to three types:

- **Condom:** (top right) A thin, stretchy latex cover that fits over a man's penis. It catches the **sperm** and stops it entering the woman's vagina.
- **Diaphragm:** A round, rubber cap that is pushed into a woman's vagina and fits over the cervix (neck of the womb) to stop sperm entering.
- **Contraceptive pill:** (right) A pill that a woman takes every day to stop her eggs from ripening so they cannot be **fertilised**.

You can buy condoms in chemists and supermarkets. But for other types of contraception, you need to go to a doctor or a family planning clinic. It's also a good idea to talk to your parents first – if you feel you can.

WEBtag Click on 'sexuality and health' for a sex health guide.

http://www.youngwomens health.org

SERIOUS STUFF 4: STIs

STIs (sexually transmitted infections) can be passed from person to person through sex. Often people don't like talking about STIs. Some can seriously damage your health or even be life-threatening, such as **HIV**, but most can be cured. If you think you have one, you must see a doctor or go to a sexual health clinic. The good news is that most STIs can be avoided by wearing a condom.

- **STIs:** chlamydia, genital warts, genital herpes, gonorrhoea, syphilis, HIV, trichomoniasis, pubic lice, scabies, HPV.

Anita says: Remember that your body is yours and no one has the right to touch you if you don't want them to. You always have the right to say 'No'.

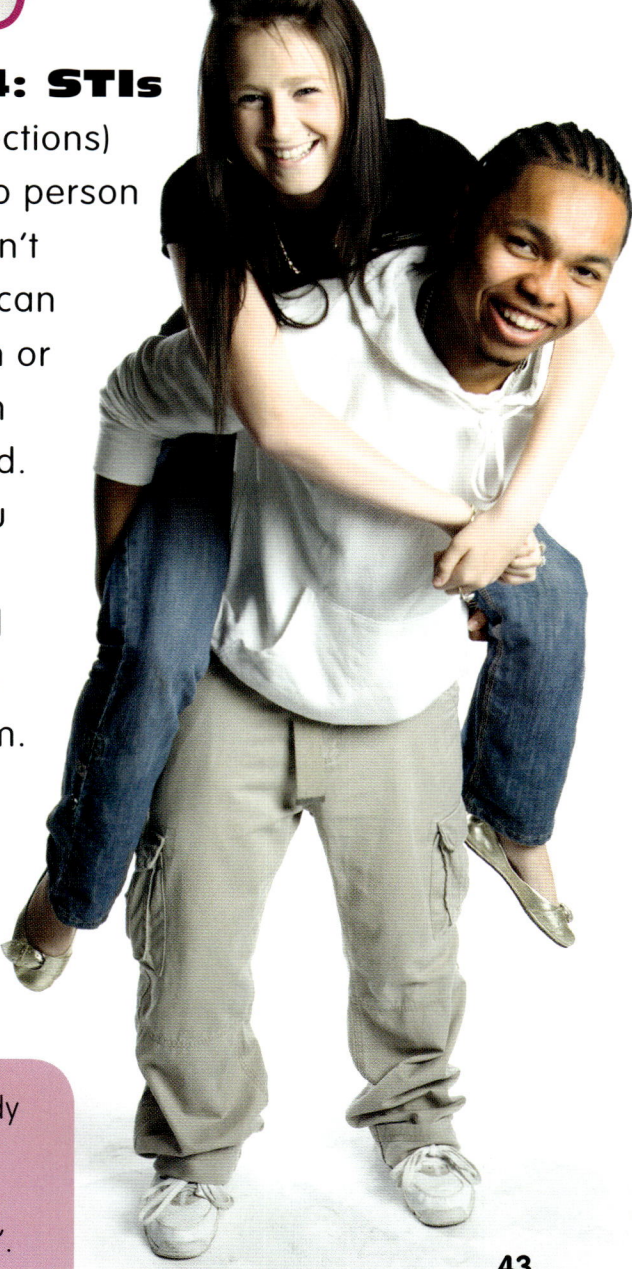

43

GLOSSARY

Approachable – someone who is easy to talk to and get along with.

Attitude – the way a person speaks, behaves and sees the world.

Blanking – completely ignoring someone or something.

Bunking off – skipping school without permission.

Confident – being very certain or sure of yourself.

Contraception – ways of preventing a woman from becoming pregnant, such as using a condom.

Crush – thinking that you are madly in love with someone, even if you have never met them.

Dumped – told that a relationship is over by the other person.

Fertilised – when an egg from a woman joins with a sperm from a man and starts to grow into a baby.

HIV – a virus that is spread via bodily fluids, especially during sex, and causes AIDs.

Hormones – chemicals inside your body that affect how your body works and behaves.

Influence – the effect that one person or thing has on another.

Jealous – feeling angry or upset when your friends or boyfriend are friendly with other people.

OTT – Over The Top – or extreme.

Peer pressure – when your friends try to make you do something, good or bad, simply because they're all doing it.

Pisces – one of the signs of the zodiac. People born under the sign of Pisces (19 February–20 March) are supposed to be sensitive.

Policy – a plan of action.

Profile page – a page you set up on a social networking site, giving details about yourself.

Puberty – when your body starts to change from a child's into an adult's, at around the ages of 9–14 years old.

Sperm – tiny cells from a man which can join with an egg cell from a woman to make a baby.

Tiff – a silly quarrel.

Tweets – messages sent on the social networking site Twitter™.

MORE WEBSITES

http://www.teengrowth.com
Teen website featuring questions and answers on a variety of health topics including STIs (or STDs – sexually transmitted diseases), contraception and sex.

http://www.childline.org.uk
UK-based helpline and information source for children looking for help. The website includes details of how you can get in touch, a games section and videos.

http://teenlineonline.org
California-based teen helpline, with an online message function and message board.

http://www.avert.org/teens.htm
Website of charity Avert, featuring information on contraception, HIV/AIDS and practical advice for teens.

http://www.kidshelp.com.au/teens
Teen pages of KidsHelpline based in Australia, providing advice and information on a range of personal health topics, from alcohol to making friends.

INDEX

14th February 16–17

attachment 8
attraction 8, 9

Bebo 37
Bieber, Justin 15
birth control, see entry for contraception
Bleu, Corbin 15
bullying 34–35, 38
bust-ups 24–25

condoms 42, 43
confidence 20, 23, 29, 44
contraception 42
crushes 10–11, 14–15
cyberbullying 38

dates 20–21
daydreams/ daydreaming 6, 11, 13
dumped 24, 25

Facebook® 36
falling in love 8–9
fancying someone 6, 8, 10, 40
first date 20
first kiss 22–23, 40
friends 7, 11, 26–33, 34, 36

HIV 43
hormones 9

in love 8–9

jealousy 18
Jonas Brothers 14

kiss/kissing 19, 22–23, 25, 40

making friends 28–29

peer pressure 32–33
puberty 9
public displays of affection 19

quiz 10–11, 26–27

relationship problems 24, 25, 28–29

secrets 20, 26
sex 40–43
STIs (sexually transmitted infections) 43
social networking sites 36–39

turn-offs 18–19
Twitter™ 37

Valentine's Day 16–17